AF407542

I Can...

- [ ] use a Capital Letter
  The cat is big.
- [ ] use spaces
- [ ] sound out words
  d-o-g = dog
- [ ] use a Period .
- [ ] Draw a picture

He is having fun, running under the sun with his new toy gun.

amusement	pistolet	courir	soleil
כיף	אקדח	לרוץ	שמש

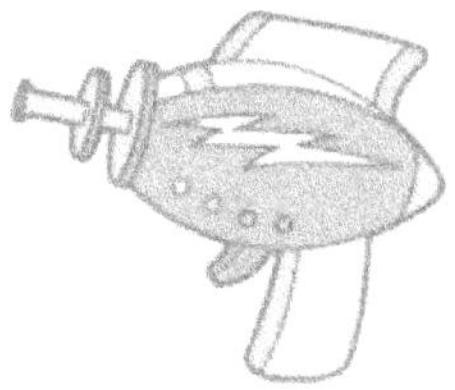

Name: ____________________ Date: ____________________

Today is: Monday Tuesday Wednesday Thursday Friday

Direction: Trace and read the sentences.

sac	chiffon	étiquette	remuer
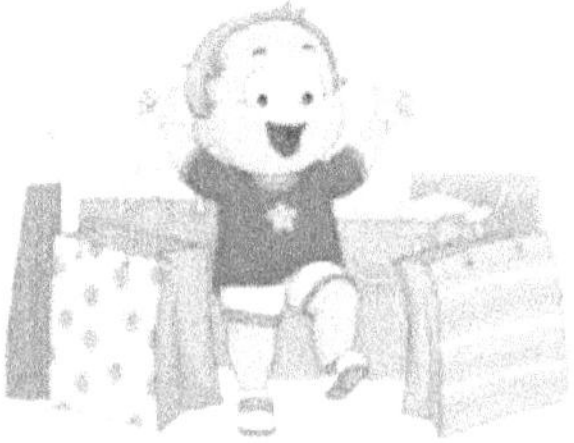		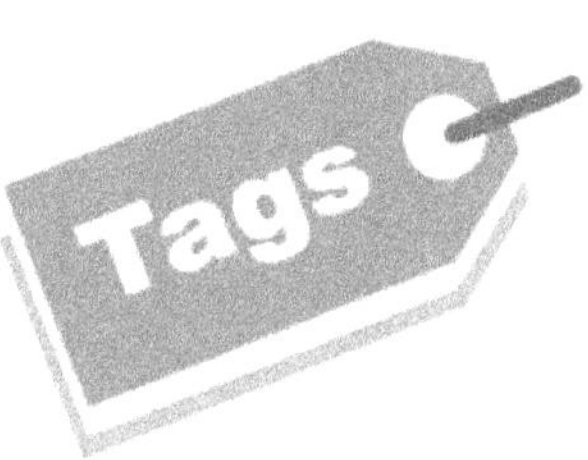	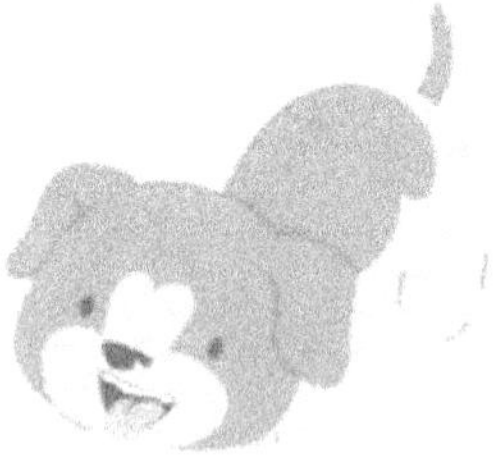
תיק	סמרטוט	תגית	מתנודד

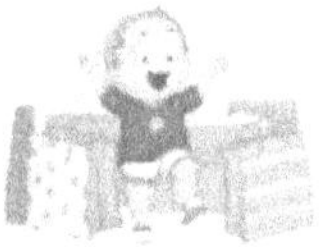

He has many bags.

I see a rag.

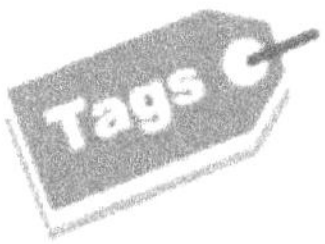

I see a tag.

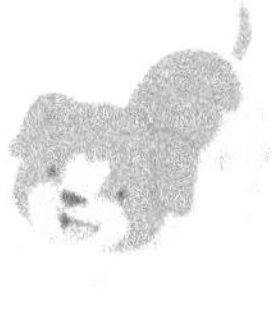

Its tail is wagging.

My Sight Word List

French - Hebrew

a	in	said
and	is	see
away	it	the
big	jump	three
blue	little	to
can	look	two
come	make	up
down	me	we
find	my	where
for	not	yellow
funny	one	you
go	day	
help	play	
here	red	
I	run	

Name: ______________________ Date: ______________________

Today is: Monday | Tuesday | Wednesday | Thursday | Friday

Direction: Trace and read the sentences.

amusement	pistolet	courir	soleil
	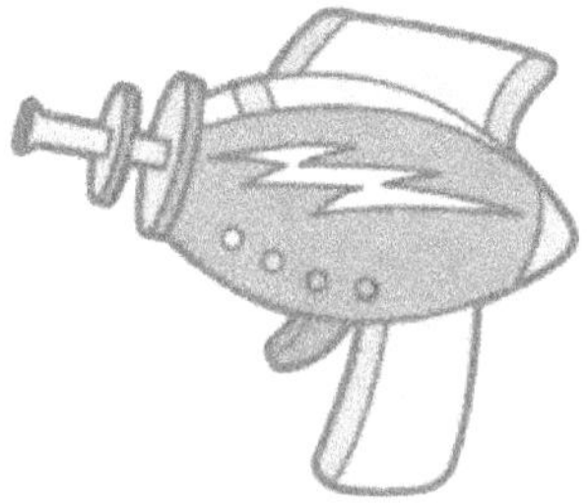		
כיף	אקדח	לרוץ	שמש

They are having fun.

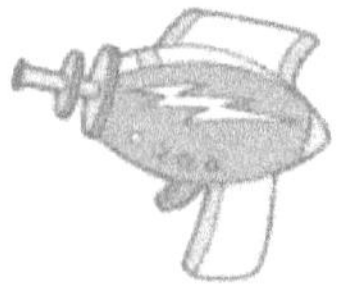

He has a gun.

The bear is running.

The sun is smiling.

The bag on the rag has
a blue tag which made
the dog's tail wag.

sac	chiffon	étiquette	remuer
תיק	סמרטוט	תג׳ית	מתנודד

Name: ____________________ Date: ____________________

Today is: Monday Tuesday Wednesday Thursday Friday

Direction: Trace and read the sentences.

canettes	homme	la poêle	van
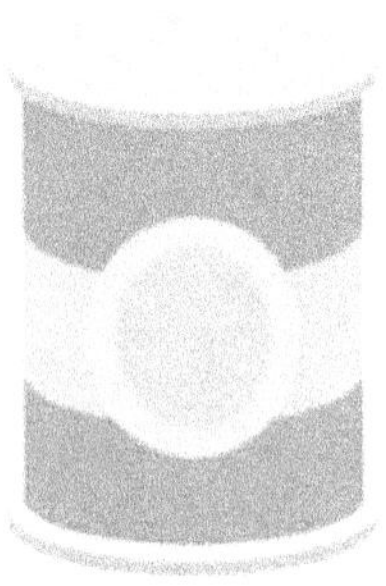			
פחיות	איש	מחבת	ואן

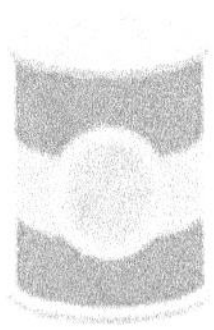

I see a can of soda.

The man is happy.

The pan is dirty.

I see a big van.

Name _______________________

Draw a Picture

I Can...

- [ ] use a Capital Letter
  <u>T</u>he cat is big.

- [ ] use spaces

- [ ] sound out words
  d-o-g = dog

- [ ] use a Period .

- [ ] Draw a picture

The man who was driving
a van ran over a can
and a pan.

canettes	homme	la poêle	van
פחיות	איש	מחבת	ואן

Name: ______________________ Date: ______________________

Today is: Monday | Tuesday | Wednesday | Thursday | Friday

Direction: Trace and read the sentences.

couper	intestin	cabane	écrou

גזירה	בטן	צריף	אגוז

He cut his nails.

He has a gut.

This is a small hut.

It is holding a nut.

A boy swallowed a nut and
it got stuck in his belly.
He had to get his gut
cut open in the hut.

couper	intestin	cabane	écrou
גזירה	בטן	צריף	אגוז

Name: ______________________ Date: ______________________

Today is: Monday | Tuesday | Wednesday | Thursday | Friday

Direction: Trace and read the sentences.

graisse	chat	chapeau	tapis

שמן	חתול	כובע	מחצלת

I see a fat dog.

This is my little cat.

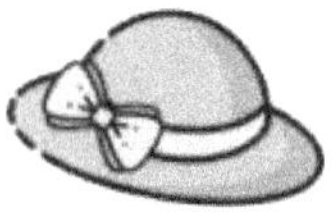

I like this hat.

I see a big mat.

Name ______________________

Draw a Picture

I Can...

- ☐ use a Capital Letter
  <u>T</u>he cat is big.

- ☐ use spaces

- ☐ sound out words
  d-o-g = dog

- ☐ use a Period .

- ☐ Draw a picture

The fat cat laid on the
mat that was a hat
pattern.

graisse	chat	chapeau	tapis
שמן	חתול	כובע	מחצלת

Name: _____________________ Date: _____________

Today is: Monday Tuesday Wednesday

Thursday Friday

Direction: Trace and read the sentences.

taxi	laboratoire	languette	crabe
מונית	מעבדה	כרטיסייה	סרטן

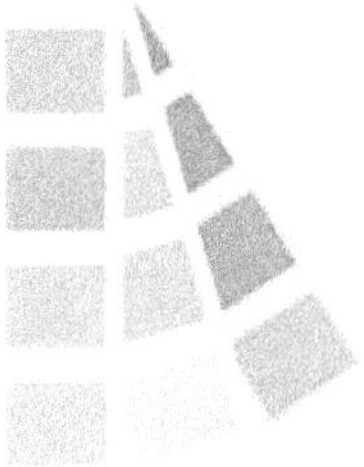

The cab is fast.

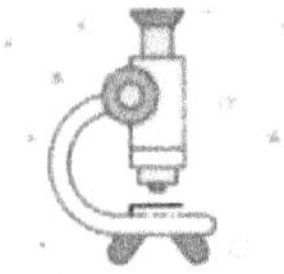

The lab is exciting.

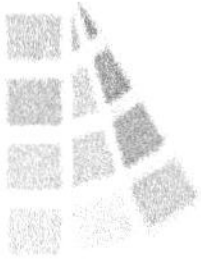

The tab is long.

We found a crab.

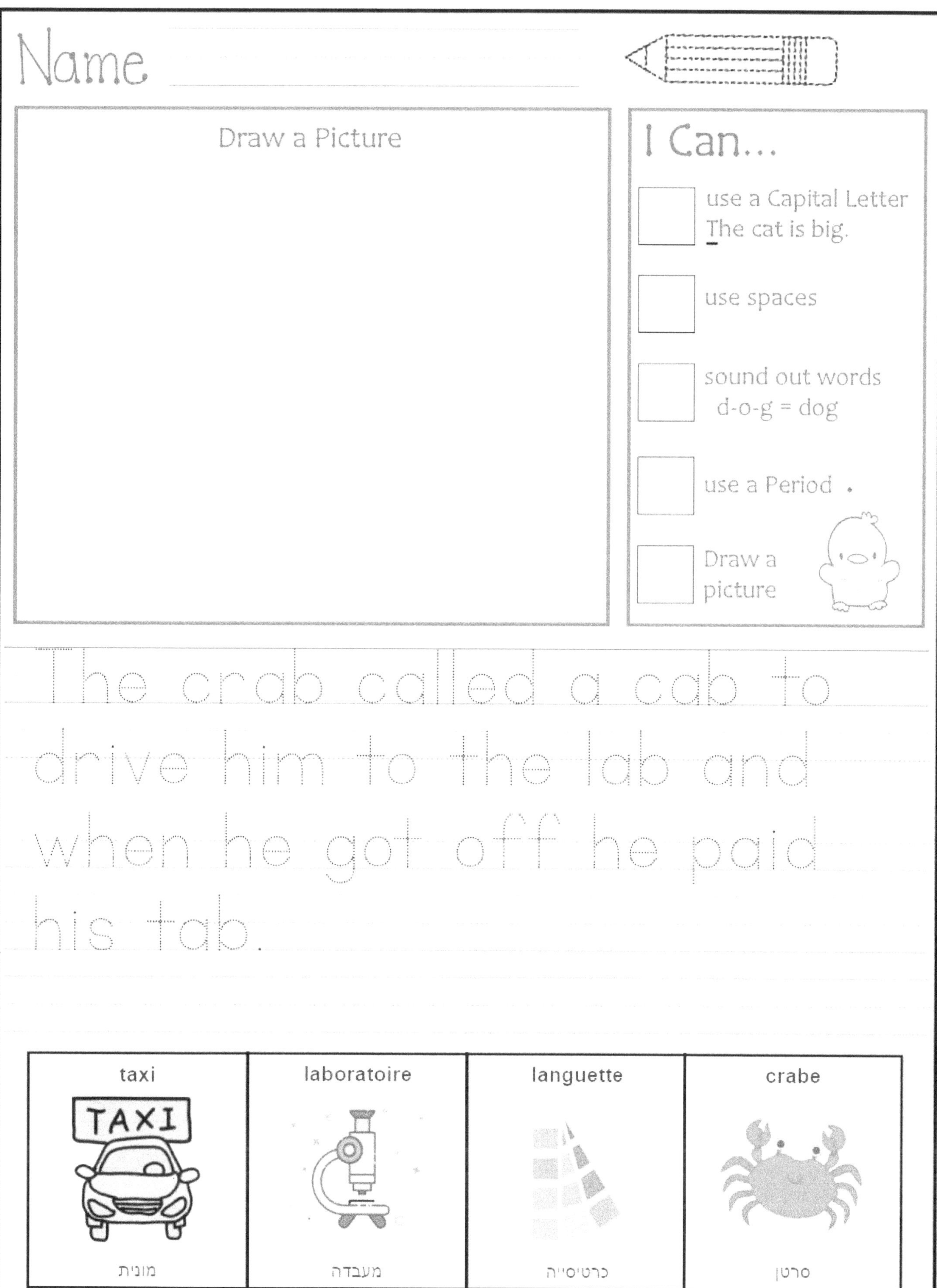

Name

Draw a Picture

I Can...

use a Capital Letter
The cat is big.

use spaces

sound out words
d-o-g = dog

use a Period .

Draw a
picture

The crab called a cab to
drive him to the lab and
when he got off he paid
his tab.

taxi
laboratoire
languette
crabe

מונית
מעבדה
כרטיסייה
סרטן

Name: ____________________ Date: ____________________

Today is: Monday | Tuesday | Wednesday | Thursday | Friday

Direction: Trace and read the sentences.

jambon	confiture	mouton	palourde
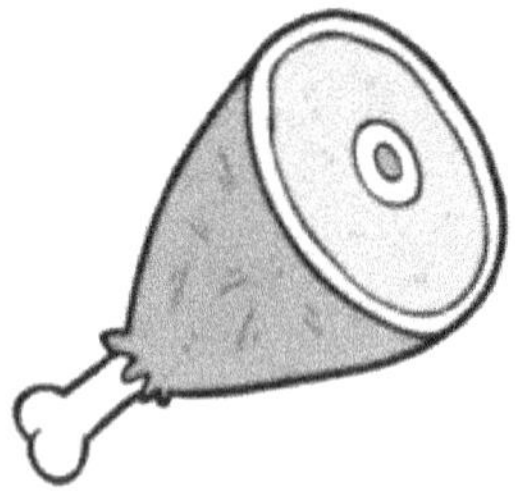	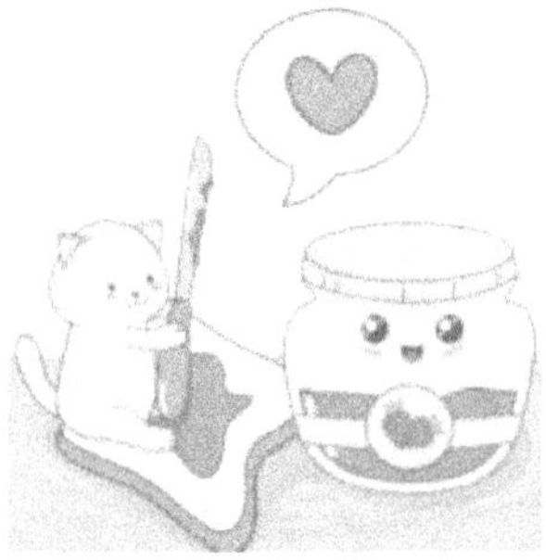	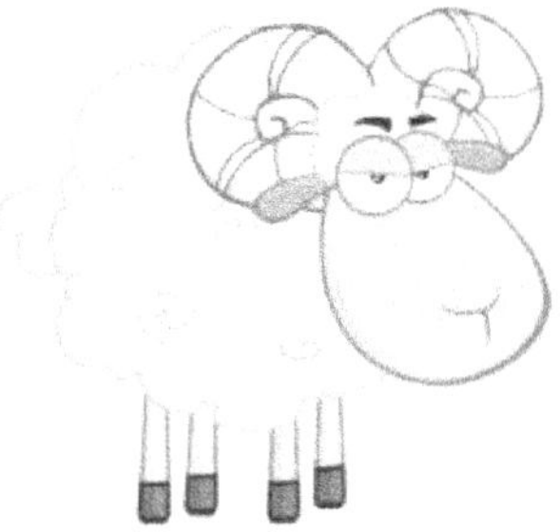	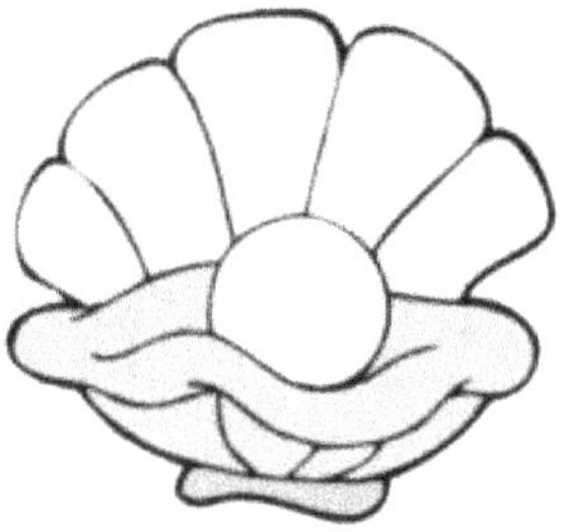
חזיר	ריבה	כבשים	צדף

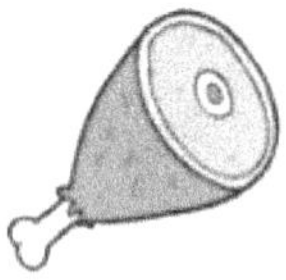

I like to eat ham.

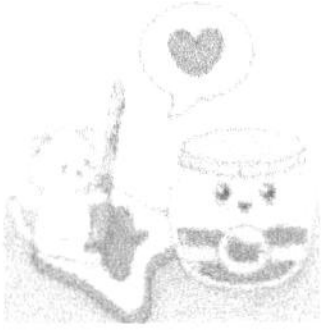

We like to eat jam.

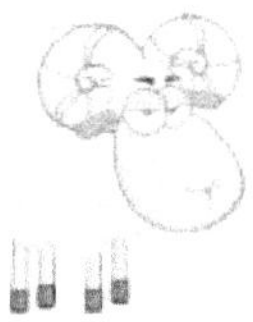

The ram is big.

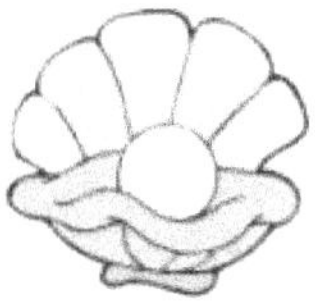

The clam is pretty.

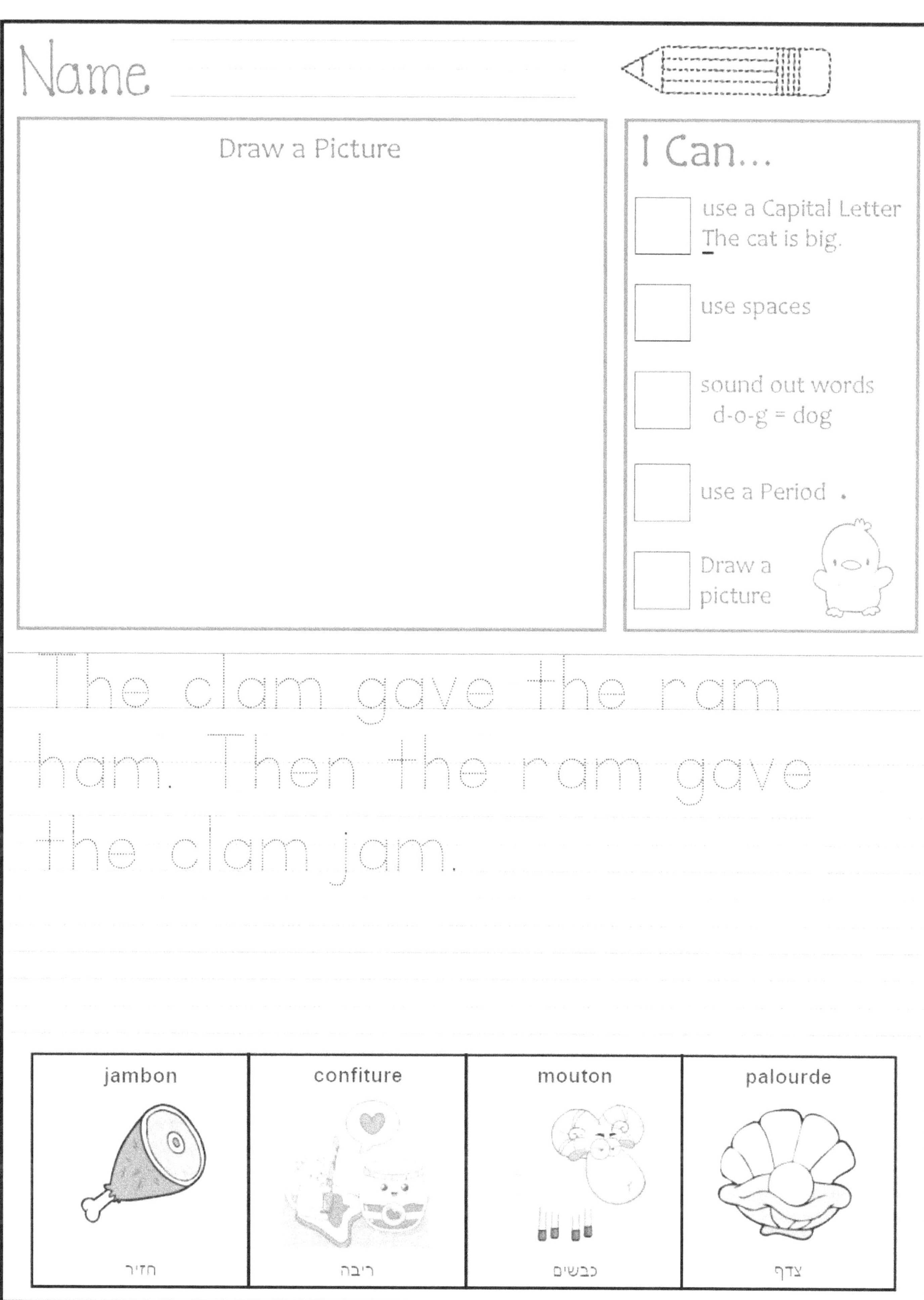

Name
Draw a Picture
I Can...
use a Capital Letter
The cat is big.
use spaces
sound out words
d-o-g = dog
use a Period .
Draw a
picture
The clam gave the ram
ham. Then the ram gave
the clam jam.
jambon
confiture
mouton
palourde
חזיר
ריבה
כבשים
צדף

Name: _______________ Date: _______________

Today is: | Monday | Tuesday | Wednesday |
| Thursday | Friday |

Direction: Trace and read the sentences.

lit	de premier plan	rouge	mariage
מיטה	מוביל	אדום	חתונה

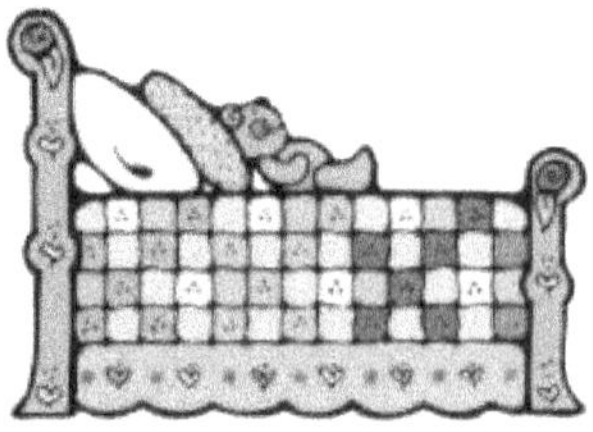

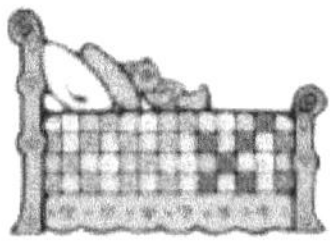

This is my little bed.

He led us to safety.

The apple is red.

He asks her to wed.

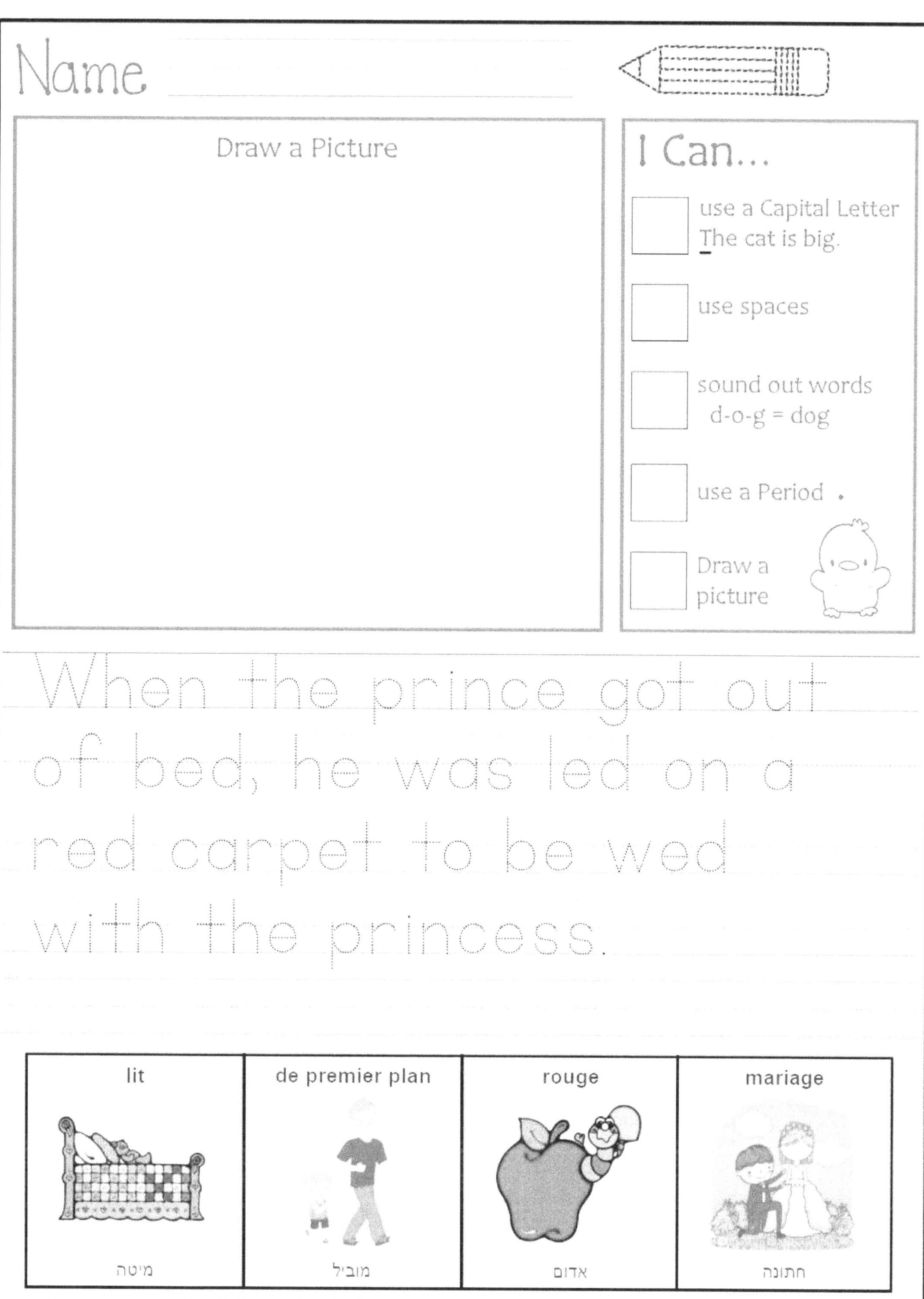

Name ______________________

Draw a Picture

I Can...

- [ ] use a Capital Letter
  The cat is big.
- [ ] use spaces
- [ ] sound out words
  d-o-g = dog
- [ ] use a Period .
- [ ] Draw a picture

When the prince got out of bed, he was led on a red carpet to be wed with the princess.

lit	de premier plan	rouge	mariage
מיטה	מוביל	אדום	חתונה

Name: ______________________ Date: ______________________

Today is: Monday | Tuesday | Wednesday | Thursday | Friday

Direction: Trace and read the sentences.

mauvais	papa	furieux	triste

רע	אבא	כועס	עצוב

This apple is bad.

My dad is very kind.

The reindeer is mad.

The little cat is sad.

Draw a Picture

I Can...

- ☐ use a Capital Letter
  The cat is big.
- ☐ use spaces
- ☐ sound out words
  d-o-g = dog
- ☐ use a Period .
- ☐ Draw a picture

I was bad so my dad got mad and now I am so sad.

mauvais	papa	furieux	triste
רע	אבא	כועס	עצוב

Name: _______________ Date: _______________

Today is:

| Monday | Tuesday | Wednesday |

| Thursday | Friday |

Direction: Trace and read the sentences.

animal den	poule	écuries	dix
den	תרנגולת	אורוות	עשר

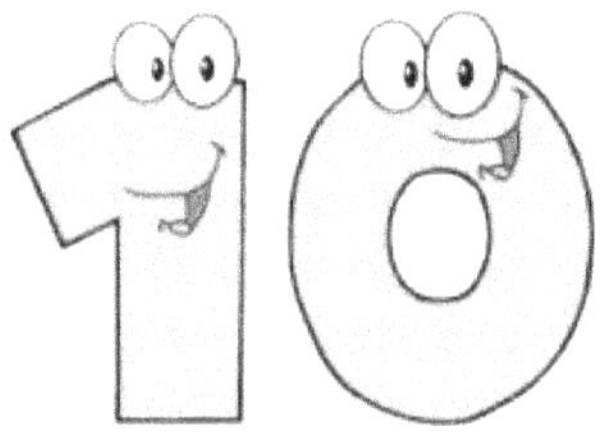

It is a den.

The hens lay eggs.

She has a good pen.

The ten is smiling.

The hen that lived in the
pen laid ten eggs
in her den.

animal den	poule	écuries	dix
den	תרנגולת	אורוות	עשר

Name: _________________________ Date: _________________

Today is: [Monday] [Tuesday] [Wednesday]
[Thursday] [Friday]

Direction: Trace and read the sentences.

gommeux	maman	somme	tambour
מסטיק	אמא	סכום	תוף

I like to chew gum.

My mum is kind!

I can do a sum!

The drum is big.

Name

Draw a Picture

I Can...

- ☐ use a Capital Letter
  The cat is big.
- ☐ use spaces
- ☐ sound out words
  d-o-g = dog
- ☐ use a Period .
- ☐ Draw a picture

Mum was chewing gum while figuring out the sum of the drum's price.

gommeux	maman	somme	tambour
מסטיק	אמא	סכום	תוף

Name: _______________________ Date: _______________________

Today is: Monday   Tuesday   Wednesday

Thursday   Friday

Direction: Trace and read the sentences.

offre	cacher	enfant	couvercle
הצעת מחיר	להתחבא	ילד	מכסה

He likes to bid.

He is hiding.

The kid like to play.

I see a lid.

Draw a Picture

I Can...

- [ ] use a Capital Letter
  The cat is big.
- [ ] use spaces
- [ ] sound out words
  d-o-g = dog
- [ ] use a Period .
- [ ] Draw a picture

The kid bid a lid for one hundred dollars then hid from his mad parents.

offre	cacher	enfant	couvercle
הצעת מחיר	להתחבא	ילד	מכסה

Name: ______________________ Date: ______________________

Today is: Monday | Tuesday | Wednesday | Thursday | Friday

Direction: Trace and read the sentences.

gros	creuser	porc	perruque

גדול	לחפור	חזיר	פאה

That is a big pencil.

He will dig up a hole.

The pig is fat.

She puts on a wig.

The big pig went to dig
in the mud for his wig.

gros	creuser	porc	perruque
גדול	לחפור	חזיר	פאה

Name: _____________ Date: _____________

Today is: Monday Tuesday Wednesday

Thursday Friday

Direction: Trace and read the sentences.

poubelle	ailette	épingle	gagner
RECYCLE			
סל	סנפיר	סיכה	לנצח

It is a recycle bin.

The shark has a fin.

The pin is pointy.

He won the match.

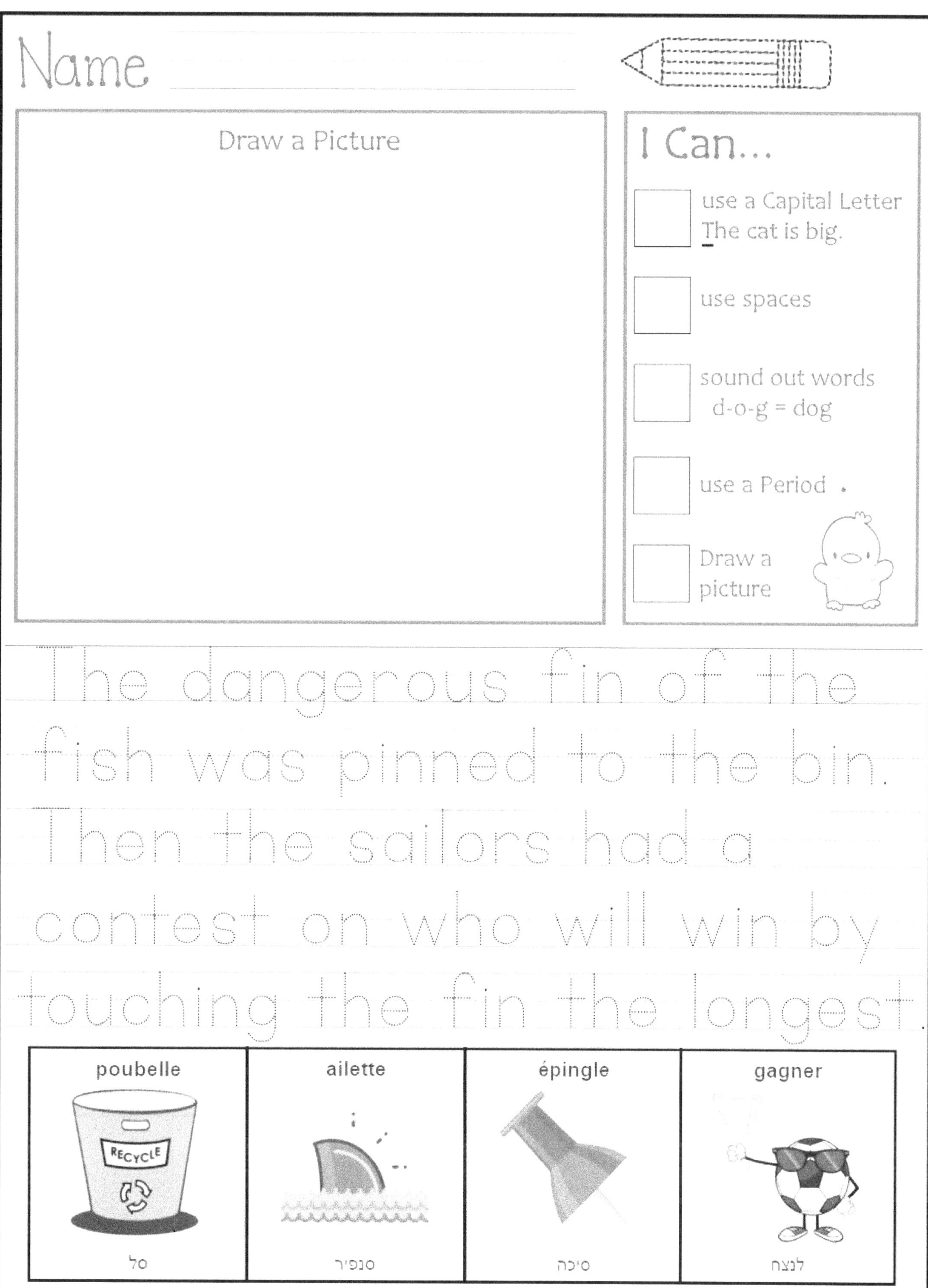

Name
Draw a Picture
I Can...
use a Capital Letter
The cat is big.
use spaces
sound out words
d-o-g = dog
use a Period .
Draw a picture
The dangerous fin of the fish was pinned to the bin. Then the sailors had a contest on who will win by touching the fin the longest.
poubelle
ailette
épingle
gagner
RECYCLE
סל
סנפיר
סיכה
לנצח

Name: _______________ Date: _______________

Today is: Monday Tuesday Wednesday
Thursday Friday

Direction: Trace and read the sentences.

hanche	lèvres	pincer	boisson
ירך	שפתיים	צביטה	לשתות

This is my hip.

Her lips are red.

It is nipping its toy.

She is sipping.

Name ____________________

Draw a Picture

I Can...

- [ ] use a Capital Letter
  The cat is big.
- [ ] use spaces
- [ ] sound out words
  d-o-g = dog
- [ ] use a Period .
- [ ] Draw a picture

The dog nipped someone
who was sipping water
with his lip.

hanche	lèvres	pincer	boisson

ירך	שפתיים	צביטה	לשתות

Name: ______________________ Date: ______________________

Today is: Monday | Tuesday | Wednesday | Thursday | Friday

Direction: Trace and read the sentences.

en forme	frappé	trousse	asseoir
		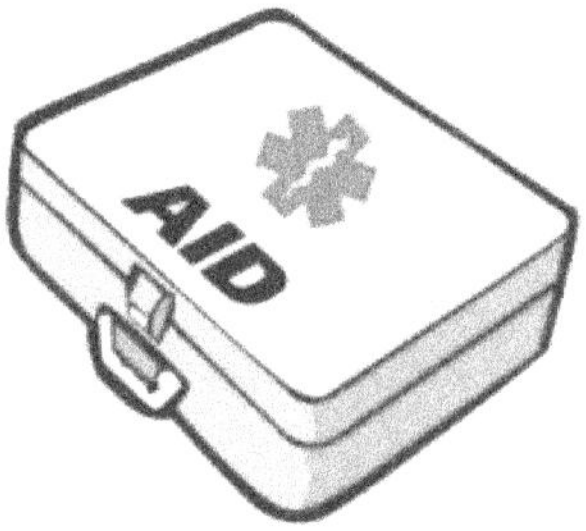	
בכושר	מכה	ערכה	לשבת

It is perfectly fit.

They hit each other.

That is a safety kit.

He is sitting.

Draw a Picture

I Can...

☐ use a Capital Letter
The cat is big.

☐ use spaces

☐ sound out words
d-o-g = dog

☐ use a Period .

☐ Draw a picture

The fit doctor sat then was hit by a kit.

en forme	frappé	trousse	asseoir
בכושר	מכה	ערכה	לשבת

Name: ____________________ Date: ____________________

Today is: Monday Tuesday Wednesday Thursday Friday

Direction: Trace and read the sentences.

blé	emploi	rob	pleurer

תירס	עבודה	לשדוד	בוכה

 I ate corn on the cob.

 This is my job.

 He is robbing.

 The girl is sobbing.

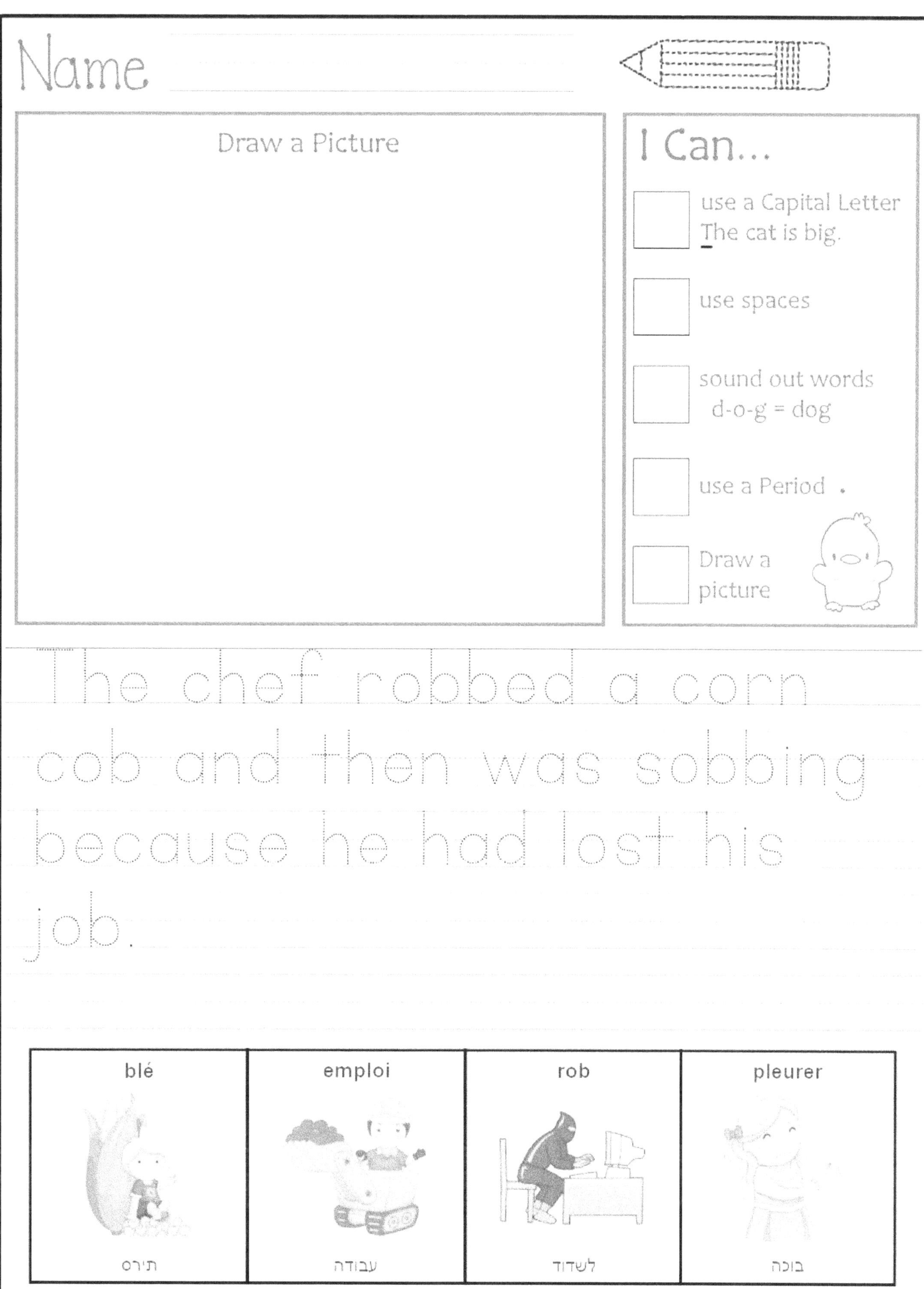

Name ___________

Draw a Picture

I Can...

- ☐ use a Capital Letter
  <u>T</u>he cat is big.
- ☐ use spaces
- ☐ sound out words
  d-o-g = dog
- ☐ use a Period .
- ☐ Draw a picture

The chef robbed a corn cob and then was sobbing because he had lost his job.

blé	emploi	rob	pleurer
תירס	עבודה	לשדוד	בוכה

Name: ______________________ Date: ______________________

Today is: Monday | Tuesday | Wednesday | Thursday | Friday

Direction: Trace and read the sentences.

chien	porc	le jogging	bois
			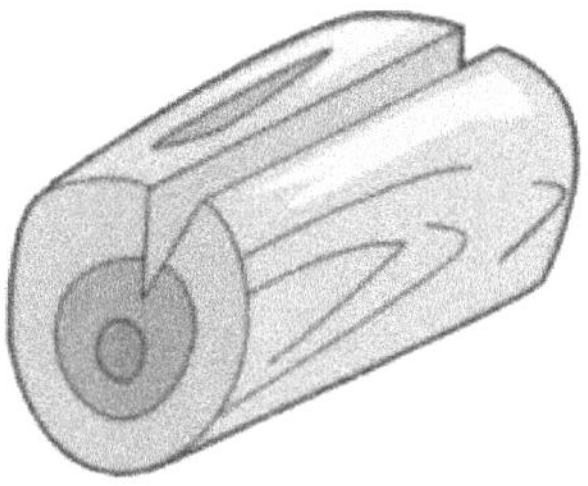
כלב	חזיר	ריצה קלה	עץ

The dog is thrilled.

The hog is big.

She is jogging.

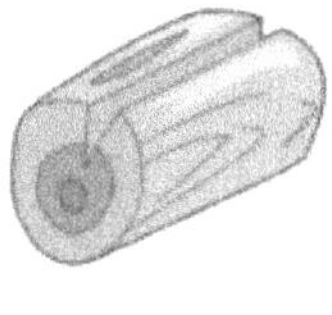

The log is small.

Name ____________________

Draw a Picture

I Can...

- [ ] use a Capital Letter
  The cat is big.

- [ ] use spaces

- [ ] sound out words
  d-o-g = dog

- [ ] use a Period .

- [ ] Draw a picture

The dog and the hog went for a jog but then tripped on a log.

chien	porc	le jogging	bois
כלב	חזיר	ריצה קלה	עץ

Name: ____________________ Date: ____________________

Today is: Monday Tuesday Wednesday Thursday Friday

Direction: Trace and read the sentences.

punaise	étreinte	cruche	agresser
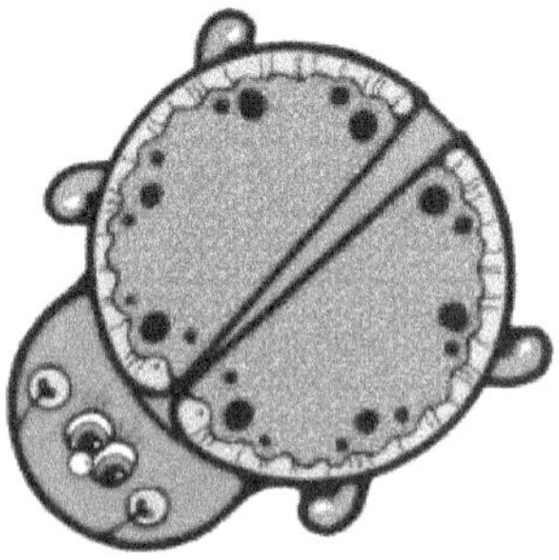			
חרק	חיבוק	כד	ספל

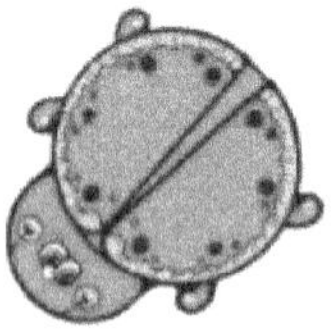 The bug is colorful.

 She is hugging.

 The jug has milk in it.

 He has a mug.

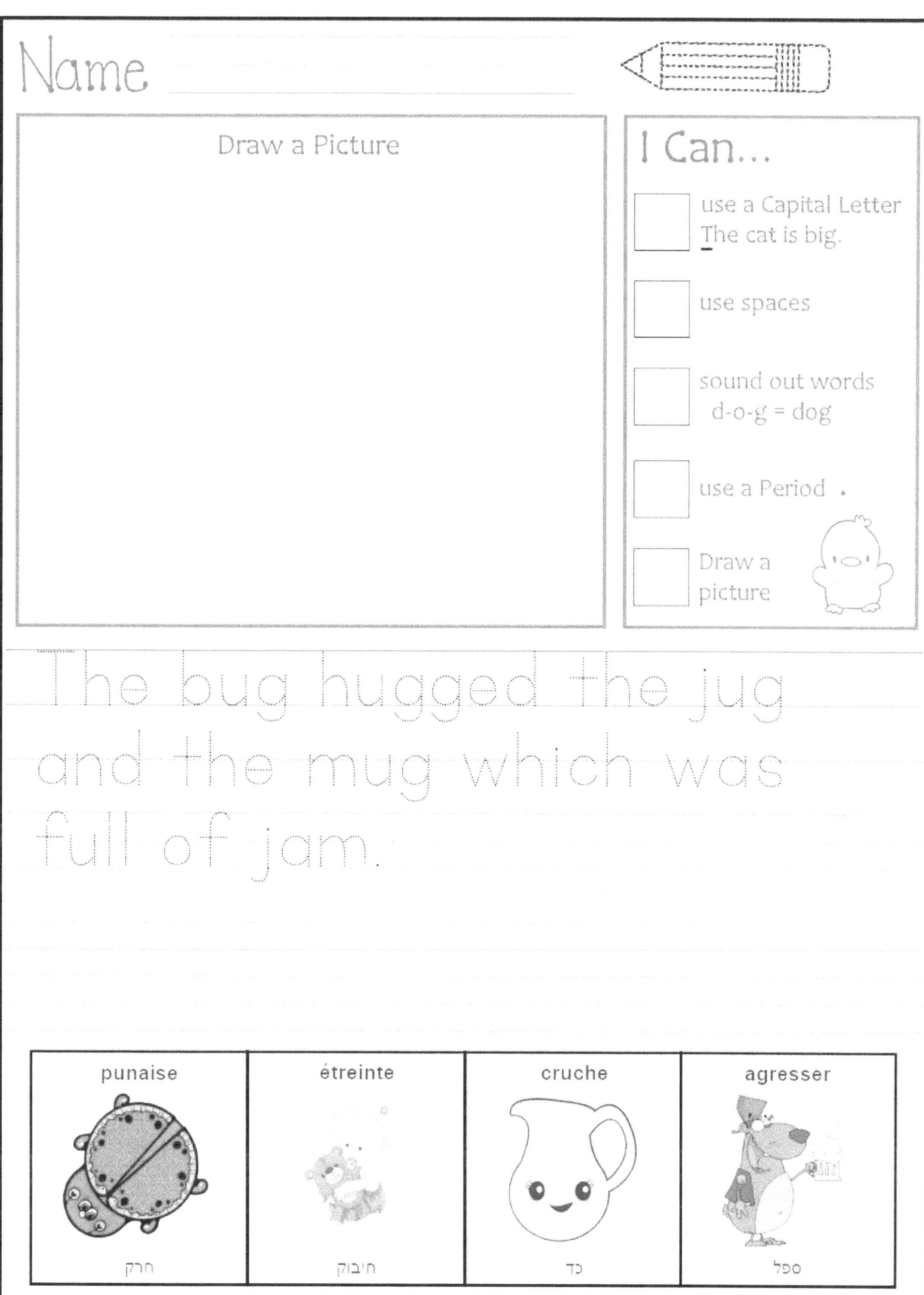

Name

Draw a Picture

I Can...

use a Capital Letter
The cat is big.

use spaces

sound out words
d-o-g = dog

use a Period .

Draw a
picture

The bug hugged the jug
and the mug which was
full of jam.

punaise
חרק

étreinte
חיבוק

cruche
כד

agresser
ספל

Name: ______________________ Date: ______________________

Today is: Monday | Tuesday | Wednesday | Thursday | Friday

Direction: Trace and read the sentences.

lit	point	chaud	pot

מיטה	נקודה	חם	סיר

This is my cot.

There are many dots.

It is very hot.

He has a plant pot.

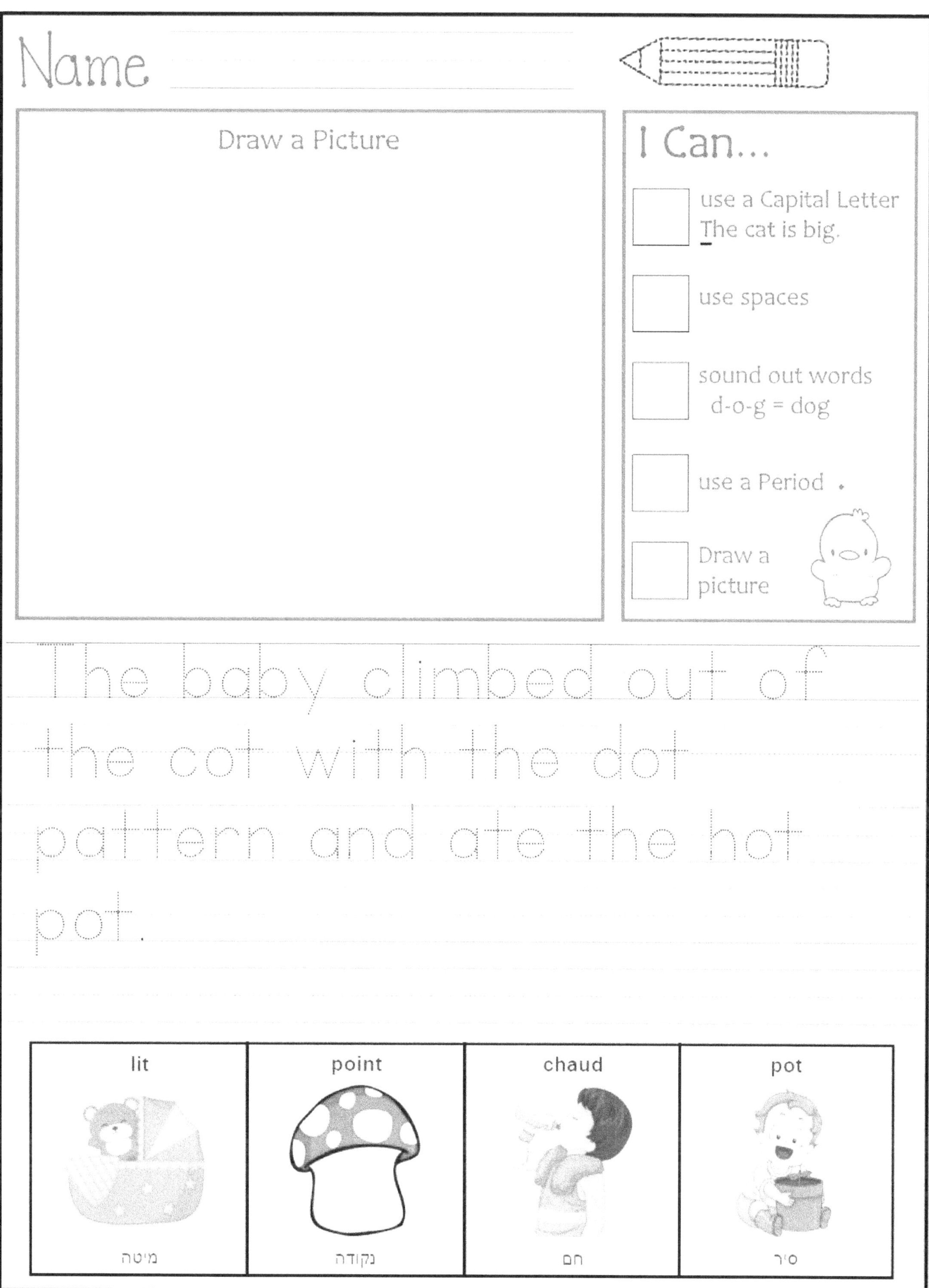

Name

Draw a Picture

I Can...

use a Capital Letter
The cat is big.

use spaces

sound out words
d-o-g = dog

use a Period .

Draw a
picture

The baby climbed out of
the cot with the dot
pattern and ate the hot
pot.

lit
מיטה

point
נקודה

chaud
חם

pot
סיר

Name: _________________________   Date: _________________

Today is: [Monday] [Tuesday] [Wednesday]
[Thursday] [Friday]

Direction: Read the words and make a sentence.

amusement	pistolet	courir	soleil
כיף	אקדח	לרוץ	שמש

Name _______________________

<table>
<tr><td>

Draw a Picture

</td><td>

I Can...

☐ use a Capital Letter
The cat is big.

☐ use spaces

☐ sound out words
d-o-g = dog

☐ use a Period .

☐ Draw a picture

</td></tr>
</table>

Name: _______________   Date: _______________

Today is: | Monday | Tuesday | Wednesday |
| Thursday | Friday |

Name: _______________________ Date: _______________

Today is: Monday   Tuesday   Wednesday
           Thursday   Friday

Direction: Read the words and make a sentence.

sac	chiffon	étiquette	remuer
תיק	סמרטוט	תגית	מתנודד

Name

Draw a Picture

I Can...

- [ ] use a Capital Letter
  The cat is big.

- [ ] use spaces

- [ ] sound out words
  d-o-g = dog

- [ ] use a Period .

- [ ] Draw a picture

Name: Date:

Today is:
        Monday   Tuesday   Wednesday
        Thursday   Friday

Name: _________________________ Date: _________________

Today is: [Monday] [Tuesday] [Wednesday]
[Thursday] [Friday]

Direction: Read the words and make a sentence.

canettes	homme	la poêle	van
פחיות	איש	מחבת	ואן

Name

Draw a Picture

I Can...

☐ use a Capital Letter
The cat is big.

☐ use spaces

☐ sound out words
d-o-g = dog

☐ use a Period .

☐ Draw a picture

Name: ___________________   Date: ___________________

Today is: Monday   Tuesday   Wednesday   Thursday   Friday

Name: _______________________ Date: _______________________

Today is:

| Monday | Tuesday | Wednesday |

| Thursday | Friday |

Direction: Read the words and make a sentence.

couper	intestin	cabane	écrou
גזירה	בטן	צריף	אגוז

Name ____________________

Draw a Picture

I Can...

☐ use a Capital Letter
The cat is big.

☐ use spaces

☐ sound out words
d-o-g = dog

☐ use a Period .

☐ Draw a
picture

Name: ___________________ Date: ___________

Today is:

| Monday | Tuesday | Wednesday |
| Thursday | Friday |

Name: _______________________ Date: _______________

Today is: Monday Tuesday Wednesday
Thursday Friday

Direction: Read the words and make a sentence.

graisse	chat	chapeau	tapis
שמן	חתול	כובע	מחצלת

Name _______________________

Draw a Picture

I Can...

☐ use a Capital Letter
The cat is big.

☐ use spaces

☐ sound out words
d-o-g = dog

☐ use a Period .

☐ Draw a picture

Name: _______________________ Date: _______________________

Today is: | Monday | Tuesday | Wednesday |
| Thursday | Friday |

Name: _______________   Date: _______________

Today is: [Monday] [Tuesday] [Wednesday]
[Thursday] [Friday]

Direction: Read the words and make a sentence.

taxi	laboratoire	languette	crabe
מונית	מעבדה	כרטיסייה	סרטן

Name

Draw a Picture

I Can...

- [ ] use a Capital Letter
  The cat is big.

- [ ] use spaces

- [ ] sound out words
  d-o-g = dog

- [ ] use a Period .

- [ ] Draw a picture

Name: Date:

Today is: Monday   Tuesday   Wednesday   Thursday   Friday

Name: _______________   Date: _______________

Today is: Monday   Tuesday   Wednesday
Thursday   Friday

Direction: Read the words and make a sentence.

jambon	confiture	mouton	palourde
חזיר	ריבה	כבשים	צדף

Name _______________________

Draw a Picture

I Can...

☐ use a Capital Letter
The cat is big.

☐ use spaces

☐ sound out words
d-o-g = dog

☐ use a Period .

☐ Draw a
picture

Name:
Date:
Today is:
Monday
Tuesday
Wednesday
Thursday
Friday

Name: _________________ Date: _________________

Today is:

Monday Tuesday Wednesday

Thursday Friday

Direction: Read the words and make a sentence.

lit	de premier plan	rouge	mariage
מיטה	מוביל	אדום	חתונה

Name

Draw a Picture

I Can...

- [ ] use a Capital Letter
  The cat is big.

- [ ] use spaces

- [ ] sound out words
  d-o-g = dog

- [ ] use a Period .

- [ ] Draw a picture

Name: _______________ Date: _______________

Today is: Monday Tuesday Wednesday Thursday Friday

Name: _______________ Date: _______________

Today is: | Monday | Tuesday | Wednesday |
| Thursday | Friday |

Direction: Read the words and make a sentence.

mauvais	papa	furieux	triste
רע	אבא	כועס	עצוב

Name ___________________________

Draw a Picture

I Can...

☐ use a Capital Letter
The cat is big.

☐ use spaces

☐ sound out words
d-o-g = dog

☐ use a Period .

☐ Draw a
picture

Name: _______________ Date: _______________

Today is:

Monday | Tuesday | Wednesday

Thursday | Friday

Name: _______________________ Date: _______________________

Today is: Monday   Tuesday   Wednesday
           Thursday   Friday

Direction: Read the words and make a sentence.

animal den	poule	écuries	dix
den	תרנגולת	אורוות	עשר

Name

Draw a Picture

I Can...

☐ use a Capital Letter
The cat is big.

☐ use spaces

☐ sound out words
d-o-g = dog

☐ use a Period .

☐ Draw a picture

Name: Date:

Today is: Monday   Tuesday   Wednesday

Thursday   Friday

Name: _________________________ Date: _________________

Today is: Monday Tuesday Wednesday Thursday Friday

Direction: Read the words and make a sentence.

gommeux	maman	somme	tambour
מסטיק	אמא	סכום	תוף

Name

Draw a Picture

I Can...

- [ ] use a Capital Letter
  The cat is big.

- [ ] use spaces

- [ ] sound out words
  d-o-g = dog

- [ ] use a Period .

- [ ] Draw a
  picture

Name: ___________   Date: ___________

Today is: Monday   Tuesday   Wednesday
           Thursday   Friday

Name: ______________________   Date: ______________

Today is: [Monday] [Tuesday] [Wednesday]
[Thursday] [Friday]

Direction: Read the words and make a sentence.

offre	cacher	enfant	couvercle
הצעת מחיר	להתחבא	ילד	מכסה

Draw a Picture

I Can...

- [ ] use a Capital Letter
  The cat is big.

- [ ] use spaces

- [ ] sound out words
  d-o-g = dog

- [ ] use a Period .

- [ ] Draw a picture

Name: _______________ Date: _______________

Today is: Monday Tuesday Wednesday Thursday Friday

Name: _______________________ Date: _______________

Today is: Monday   Tuesday   Wednesday

Thursday   Friday

Direction: Read the words and make a sentence.

gros	creuser	porc	perruque
גדול	לחפור	חזיר	פאה

Name ___________________________

Draw a Picture

I Can...

- [ ] use a Capital Letter
The cat is big.

- [ ] use spaces

- [ ] sound out words
d-o-g = dog

- [ ] use a Period .

- [ ] Draw a picture

Name: _______________   Date: _______________

Today is: [Monday] [Tuesday] [Wednesday]
           [Thursday] [Friday]

Name: _______________________ Date: _______________

Today is: [Monday] [Tuesday] [Wednesday]
          [Thursday] [Friday]

Direction: Read the words and make a sentence.

poubelle	ailette	épingle	gagner
סל	סנפיר	סיכה	לנצח

Name _______________________

Draw a Picture

I Can...

- [ ] use a Capital Letter
  The cat is big.

- [ ] use spaces

- [ ] sound out words
  d-o-g = dog

- [ ] use a Period .

- [ ] Draw a picture

Name: Date:

Today is: [Monday] [Tuesday] [Wednesday]
           [Thursday] [Friday]

Name: _______________________ Date: _______________

Today is: | Monday | Tuesday | Wednesday |
| Thursday | Friday |

Direction: Read the words and make a sentence.

hanche	lèvres	pincer	boisson
ירך	שפתיים	צביטה	לשתות

Name

Draw a Picture

I Can...

- [ ] use a Capital Letter
  The cat is big.

- [ ] use spaces

- [ ] sound out words
  d-o-g = dog

- [ ] use a Period .

- [ ] Draw a picture

Name: _______________   Date: _______________

Today is: Monday Tuesday Wednesday Thursday Friday

Name: _______________________ Date: _______________

Today is: [Monday] [Tuesday] [Wednesday]
          [Thursday] [Friday]

Direction: Read the words and make a sentence.

en forme	frappé	trousse	asseoir
בכושר	מכה	ערכה	לשבת

Name

Draw a Picture

I Can...

☐ use a Capital Letter
The cat is big.

☐ use spaces

☐ sound out words
d-o-g = dog

☐ use a Period .

☐ Draw a picture

Name: Date:

Today is: Monday   Tuesday   Wednesday

Thursday   Friday

blé	emploi	rob	pleurer
תירס	עבודה	לשדוד	בוכה

Name

Draw a Picture

I Can...

- [ ] use a Capital Letter
  The cat is big.

- [ ] use spaces

- [ ] sound out words
  d-o-g = dog

- [ ] use a Period .

- [ ] Draw a picture

Name: Date:

Today is:

Name: _______________________ Date: _______________

Today is: Monday   Tuesday   Wednesday

Thursday   Friday

Direction: Read the words and make a sentence.

chien	porc	le jogging	bois
כלב	חזיר	ריצה קלה	עץ

Name

Draw a Picture

I Can...

☐ use a Capital Letter
The cat is big.

☐ use spaces

☐ sound out words
d-o-g = dog

☐ use a Period .

☐ Draw a picture

Name: Date:

Today is:

Monday   Tuesday   Wednesday

Thursday   Friday

Name: _______________   Date: _______________

Today is:

Direction: Read the words and make a sentence.

punaise	étreinte	cruche	agresser
חרק	חיבוק	כד	ספל

Name

Draw a Picture

I Can...

☐ use a Capital Letter
The cat is big.

☐ use spaces

☐ sound out words
d-o-g = dog

☐ use a Period .

☐ Draw a picture

Name: _______________   Date: _______________

Today is: Monday   Tuesday   Wednesday   Thursday   Friday

Name: _______________________   Date: _______________

Today is: [Monday] [Tuesday] [Wednesday]
           [Thursday] [Friday]

Direction: Read the words and make a sentence.

lit	point	chaud	pot
מיטה	נקודה	חם	סיר

Name

Draw a Picture

I Can...

- [ ] use a Capital Letter
  The cat is big.

- [ ] use spaces

- [ ] sound out words
  d-o-g = dog

- [ ] use a Period .

- [ ] Draw a picture

Name: _________________   Date: _________

Today is: Monday Tuesday Wednesday Thursday Friday